FAMILY

FAMILY

Reflections and Memories

JANE P. RESNICK

SMITHMARK

This edition published in 1995
by Smithmark Publishers, Inc., 16 East 32nd Street, New York, NY 10016.

SMITHMARK books are available for bulk purchase for sales promotion and premium use. For details write or call the manager of special sales, SMITHMARK Publishers, Inc., 16 East 32nd Street, New York, NY 10016; 212-532-6600.

Cover design by Joyce C. Weston
Printed in the United States of America

10 9 8 7 6 5 4 3 2 1

ACKNOWLEDGMENTS

The Hartford Courant/Northeast Magazine for selected excerpts from "My Mother's House" by Jane Parker Resnick, May 15, 1985. Reprinted with permission.

The New York Times Company for excerpts from "Everything Old Is New Again" by Jane Parker Resnick, June 9, 1985. Copyright © 1985 by The New York Times Company. Reprinted with permission.

To Allison and Jill,
who in my heart are children still

A SENSE OF
WONDER

A Sense of Wonder

*T*he sense of wonder I felt when my first child was born was so great that I thought the euphoria would last a lifetime. Actually, the first three months *felt* like a lifetime. It wasn't long before I was losing my sense of wonder and getting bogged down in the less than wonderful details of diaper pails and doctor visits and the sleeping habits of an infant with absolutely no respect for the normal rhythm of night and day.

But for her grandmothers, the magic never stopped. The baby, wakeful and restless, cried often and with gusto. My mother turned her ear to the shrieks that turned my stomach and pronounced the ungodly noise, "that sweet sound." Astounded, I wondered how musical she would find her tones at 3:00 a.m. — right after the 2:00 a.m. feeding.

My mother-in-law waxed poetic about the pleasures of motherhood. "Every moment is precious," she told me, "every day a joyful experience." I imagined she wasn't speaking of the precious moments spent trying to slip pureed string beans through a baby's sealed lips. I knew she wasn't referring to the new experience of racing through the supermarkets with a small child grabbing bananas and soda bottles.

But I realized what they meant, of course, and I knew that they were right. The only trouble was that it took some distance and a little hindsight to fully appreciate their words. So, with my second child, I tried to keep my sense of wonder alive. Infant smiles and baby hugs are, indeed, moments too precious to be lost. And even when the baby cried, now and then I would think of the piercing sweetness of that sound…knowing that the grandmothers were right and that I would never hear it quite like that again.

Veteran Shopper

Shopping with young children strikes me as a peculiar kind of torture. Buying something new should be a nice experience, but somehow the idea turns out to be a lot more pleasant than the reality. Some kids would rather go to the dentist than a department store while others behave as if money is irrelevant to the activity. And when it comes to choosing what to buy, there's only one rule: the worse it looks, the more they like it.

The question is: Should a girl buy a dress that gives

her the proportions of a popsicle just because she thinks she looks pretty? Doesn't her mother's opinion count at all? I don't know the answers to these questions, but I'm real familiar with the arguments.

The more important question is one of fit. When dealing with young children, how do you know if anything really fits? I've always pulled and stretched and rearranged their little bodies and then asked them, pretending they knew what they were talking about.

Shoes, in particular, were a problem. I would make a serious production out of pressing toes and marching up and down the carpet even though I realized that the new size wouldn't last any longer than the pair they'd just demolished. Still, it was their feet, so I would ask, "How do they feel?" One little veteran shopper came up with the best answer I've heard yet.

"They're OK," she said gravely looking down at her shoes, "but they're a little too tight in the crotch."

Everything Old Is New Again

I've been shopping for prom gowns with my daughter and guess what? Scarlett O'Hara is alive and well and living in the hearts of teenage-clothing designers and right there in the hearts of the girls themselves. In dressing room after dressing room, I've been zipping up oceans of taffeta, flounces of organza, and tiers of something unpleasantly synthetic to the touch that pretends to be satin.

Staggering in under yet another armload of the fluffy stuff that dreams are made of, I finally muttered, "Where did they get these things, from the closet I forgot to clean out at Grandma's?"

"You wore these?" my daughter asked incredulously. "I don't think so," she assured me. "This style is new."

New. Scarlett must have thought so, too, and Nefertiti way before her. I guess to each youthful generation every style is new. And that's probably what's been bothering me. Finding myself in a generation that's beginning to see fashions the second time around is starting to make me count the years since I wore saddle shoes, the original version so I thought.

Lately, I've been suffering from a sense of fashion déjà vu that's putting wrinkles in my mental age. Of course,

I've realized for some time now that new styles are merely inventive recreations of the old, but I must have imagined that there would be enough of the new, for me at least, to last my lifetime. At first I concluded that styles were just changing faster than before, but then it dawned on me that I'd been around long enough for the repeats.

I shouldn't have been surprised. The realization has been creeping up on me for a while now. But having a teenage daughter is sharpening my perception of a reality that is frankly more pleasant left a little fuzzy. Last fall clinched it. My daughter came home from school with this report on what "they" were wearing:

"I need a pair of plain shoes with a high heel," she told me. "They're called...pumps," she added.

"Really," I said. "Are they new?"

"Very," replied the teenage-fashion arbiter. I knew, then, that I was in trouble.

I was the girl who wore pedal pushers who now has daughters who wear cropped pants. I know there's a difference, there has to be, because I suspect there are people within the garment industry whose sole job is to make sure we can't resurrect our formerly fabulous fashions. I might be mistaken but it seems to me that pedal pushers and cropped pants are awfully close cousins to toreadors which harken back even further to a generation before mine. My mother would remember those and she and her friends would probably find it hard to believe that there are three lives in a fashion that places pants length somewhere between the ankle and the knee. But there are those before my time and those yet to come. I suppose that means I can look forward to shopping with my granddaughter for still another rendition.

A woman I loved dearly always told me that no matter how old you are, you keep feeling about 19 on the inside—only the outside changes. And I think there's some truth in that. I know I felt that way the other day in a fitting room where my daughter and I were trying on bathing suits. There I was, nineteen on the inside with a couple of decades extra on the outside. Anyway, I should have known better than to try on bathing suits in front of the same mirror as my daughter. Bikinis are back.

"Everyone"

$\mathcal{E}$veryone else does" and "everyone else has" were not the first two phrases out of my children's mouths but sometimes I can't remember anything that came before. Over the years "everyone" has progressed from watching TV all day and eating candy between meals to having a TV in their rooms and staying out all night. "Everyone" must be pretty busy.

My children have used the "everyone" argument to ask for everything from purple high top sneakers, (the world's ugliest shoes), to permission to attend a rock concert at midnight in a city two hours away, (the event least likely to occur).

"Everyone" can really be debilitating to a parent's resolve. Most of the time, however, I stick to my stock answer, dictatorial though it may be. "I don't care what 'everyone's' doing," I say just a little less firmly than I'd like to, "but *you* aren't." The guaranteed retort to this statement is "Why not?"—delivered with a look of stunned disbelief no matter how preposterous the request. The only reply that concludes the conversation—good reasons are irrelevant—is the ever articulate, "Because I said so."

Even that doesn't always work. Recently, my daughter, who has been practicing her debating skills on me more and more told me, "You can't end the discussion that way.

"Oh, yes I can," I replied smugly. "*Everyone* does."

To Each Her Own

I am often accused of being overprotective—by my husband and certainly by my children, whose greatest fear is that my fears will prevent them from doing whatever they want to do. And they want to do everything. I've even heard a hint of condemnation from friends when I've expressed my concerns, but they can't fool me. I've listened to their worries enough to know that they're no more rational than I am about trying to protect their children. The disease just manifests itself in different forms.

When my first child went to kindergarten, she had to wait for the school bus across the street, just where the road curved out of my sight. I let her go, and she quite happily marched off alone. My mother-in-law was appalled. "What," she exclaimed, "if someone *grabs* her!" The possibility had never occurred to me. But, not to worry, I told my daughter's protective grandmother. My neighbor would be at the same bus stop with her son. She wasn't afraid he'd be kidnapped. Instead, she was terrified that he'd jump in front of the bus. Each to her own fears.

One of mine is bicycles. Ever since my kids gave up their training wheels, I've been nervous when they're riding. I've driven them places I needn't have and forbidden them places I shouldn't have so that they wouldn't be sharing the road with the maniacs and idiots who drive cars. Obviously, common sense has nothing to do with this perception.

My friend feels otherwise. She is comfortable letting her children ride their bikes everywhere, on steep, serpentine streets, with heavy traffic, where the only safe vehicle, as far as I'm concerned, would be an armored tank. One year our kids needed transportation after school to a sports activity across town. The coach offered them a ride, and I gladly consented. She refused. He drove a truck and the kids had to sit in the open back—and that, said my friend, was much too dangerous.

As far as I can remember, my own mother never let me do *anything*, which means that a portion of my memory must have frozen in my brain at sixteen. "Don't you remember," she tells me, "how nervous I was the first time I let you go out with a boy in a car?" Nervous? I recall the boy.

Clearly. I can remember being nervous about what to wear, what to say, and how close to him to sit. My mother's nervousness never entered my consciousness.

What I do remember about my mother's fears is this: whenever I traveled any distance from home, she insisted that I call when I reached my destination. That call was so important to her that the routine lasted right through the honeymoon into several years of marriage. But finally, one time when I flew across the country to see my husband after an extended separation, I forgot to call. Guilt woke me in the night, and I called, but even with the time difference, I was late.

That was the last arrival call for me. But I know, if my mother had the nerve, she'd still be asking me to call. A mother's fear never really disappears. Like a tooth that only throbs now and then, it may not hurt all the time, but it's always there.

I, of course, never make my children call when they arrive somewhere. I've learned *something* from experience. I make them call when they're going to be late coming home. One minute late. My mind deals with the idea of my kids out there in the world this way: out of sight, out of mind, but the moment they're supposed to be back under my roof, and they're not, I start worrying. A lot.

I'm not going to claim that my way of coping with this fear is any better than my mother's. I'm not even going to pretend that I'm being logical or making any sense at all. When it comes to maternal protectiveness, I guess that for all of us rational behavior is beside the point.

A Sense of Responsibility

*M*ost parents want to teach their children "responsibility" and usually start their tutelage at an early age. The idea is that a boy who puts away his toys will become a man who picks up his socks. I have my doubts about this theory primarily because I don't know a single husband who is capable of lifting the lid on a clothes hamper regardless of his upbringing.

Nonetheless, I admire parents who insist upon responsible behavior from their children and then *follow through* by letting the kids suffer the consequences of their irresponsibility. A friend of mine, without exception, insists that if her children oversleep and miss the bus, they walk the three miles to school. If they don't pack their lunch, they go without a meal. If they forget the necessary clothing, they get wet in the rain, freeze in the snow, or bake in the sun.

I am in awe of her resolve, and there are moments when I am determined to follow her example. Then there's the rest of the time, most of the time, when I drive kids to school, bring them their lunches and pack extra rain gear. I often wonder whether her children will be tougher, more self-sufficient and independent than mine. Probably the ones who were born that way to begin with...will be.

The Stone Age

I'm getting used to being called old-fashioned. Having children guarantees that someone is going to think you're an old fogy no matter how young you are. I didn't realize, however, that my vocabulary would become dated before my hair turned gray. Ask me what a woman puts on her cheeks to give herself a little color and I'll answer "Rouge." Right? Wrong. "Blush" is the word. Rouge consigned me to the Stone Age. I know because my daughters told me—with a look that said I was prehistoric.

Try "phonograph." The last time I said phonograph my husband was the only one in the house who knew what I meant. "You have one in your room," I told my daughter. "I do?" she said. "Is it something that records telephone conversations?" she asked, turning pale. Evidently phonograph joined gramophone in the archives while I was napping. "Sound system" took its place.

At first, I tried to attribute this language gap to the kids' lack of knowledge rather than my lack of keeping up. But then I remembered what my mother always says when she calls on the phone and my line is busy.

"Your wire was busy," she informs me. My *wire*? Now *that's* from the Stone Age, but I'm not laughing. The only comfort to be found in this linguistic backwardness is that, as time marches forward, the next generation will be left behind, too.

"Mom"

The first time I heard my daughter call me "Mom" in *that voice*, that voice that drew a line and called for separate territory, I knew I was in trouble. "Oh, Mom," she replied to my slightest suggestion, my most innocent question. Not "Mommy" or "Mama" but "Mom" turned into a four-letter word. "Mom" stretched into two syllables, annoyance and disdain in the first and just a tinge of tolerance and forgiveness in the second.

I realized, of course, that the new pronunciation had not much to do with me personally and everything to do with her. She was just growing up. I was supposed to be grown up already, but when I heard that voice I felt like a kid, rejected and betrayed. I took it personally. I sulked. I went to bed that night grieving for the little girl I'd lost.

In the morning, she slept through her alarm and I went to wake her for school. In her sleeping face, time lapsed, and I saw the tender expression of the infant she had been. I leaned over and kissed her, touching her soft cheek to mine, not caring if she brushed me away. But waking, she hugged me and said in the voice of the child I thought was gone forever, "Good morning, Mommy."

That didn't last for long, nor should it have. Children change. And mothers, whose feelings never change, just find new ways to love them.

Social Butterfly

When my younger daughter hit her stride as a social butterfly, she never fluttered those gorgeous new wings at home. All her dazzle was for her friends. The rest of us, merely family, were treated to the personality of a caterpillar still in its cocoon—very still and virtually incommunicado. Monosyllables occasionally passed through her lips.

I figured it was just a phase, which it was. And that I would learn to live with it, which I didn't. If there really is a maternal instinct, curiosity must be a part of it. So even though restraint would have been far more admirable, I started to ask questions. In response, I got more monosyllables, which I deserved.

Still, I couldn't help myself. Once, after a school dance, I fired off a stream of what were evidently excruciatingly personal inquiries. Like: How was the dance? Did anybody dance? Does Nancy like anybody special? We were driving along in the car and she gazed out her window as if that well-traveled road were a tourist attraction.

"Why are you asking?" I heard from the back of her head.

"Just interested," I said in what I thought was my normal voice. "Besides, if I don't ask, how am I supposed to know," I added, letting my frustration make a fool of me.

"You're not supposed to know," she answered with a sigh. "You're a mother."

I wish I could say that I came up with a snappy retort but, frankly, I was left speechless. And questionless. I don't ask too many questions any more—they just whirl around in my head. I can take a hint. That day she reminded me of something special I had forgotten. I am her mother, not just her friend, and I wouldn't change that for the world.

There really is such a thing as baby talk, indecipherable and delightful. A baby cooing in the crib, the tinkle of laughter, the sudden shrieks of pleasure—these are the purest form of human speech, spontaneous, innocent, and totally unself-conscious.

The first words of my children

_____

_____

What made my baby laugh the most

_____

_____

*A baby's funny pronunciation that remains
in the family*

_____

_____

All infants are unique. Right from the beginning they have their own physical characteristics, sleeping patterns, eating habits, and idiosyncratic preferences. Objective observers might say they are peculiar or even odd, but mothers know that they are special.

My baby's odd habit

_____

_____

My baby's most noticeable physical characteristic at birth

_____

_____

Hints of preferences to come in my baby's personality

_____

_____

Letting children choose what *they* want to wear is a lot more difficult than it sounds. There's the question of appropriateness, if they're going to leave the house. And, of course, if they're going to look as cute as they can, the tops and bottoms must have some relationship. Mothers always want their children to look their best.

A child's less than wonderful (dreadful!)
favorite clothing

_____

_____

An adorable outfit I remember

_____

_____

A funny fashion fad a child had to have

_____

_____

In the comic strip "Peanuts," Linus carries a security blanket everywhere. Linus is not alone. Many children are attached to something in the very same way. Although it often seems doubtful, most will grow up and actually leave home without the object they so treasure.

My child's precious, never-to-be-separated-from object

_____

_____

My thoughts about this attachment

_____

_____

The age at which this "security blanket" was given up for good

_____

_____

Being fearful about one's children is as natural as having them. Perhaps not a moment goes by that a mother isn't worrying about one child or another. The trick is to find a balance so that little by little your fears abate and their independence grows.

A "normal" childhood activity that causes me undue fear

_____

_____

Fears I tolerate so my children can enjoy their endeavors

_____

_____

A "good" fear I feel makes sense

_____

_____

A universal explanation for changes in children's behavior is that they are going through a "phase." "Another one?" we ask ourselves. "Is there no end?" But with resignation and a smile, we realize that constant change is one of the challenges of parenthood.

A phase I remember as very trying

_____

_____

A delightful phase

_____

_____

My best phase as a mother

_____

_____

Kids can't pick their parents, but they sure can choose their friends. And that can often be appalling. The winds of change drift in with new friends, new ideas, influences, and activities. Good or bad? Sometimes that depends on the point of view, either the parent's or the child's.

A favorite among my children's friends

_____

_____

A long-lasting friendship

_____

_____

A child's surprising choice of friend

_____

_____

When a family begins, there are great expectations, only some of which life can truly grant. With resilience, optimism, and hope—which family life demands—we can always work toward creating and fulfilling new expectations.

An expectation I worked hard to fulfill

_____

_____

An unrealistic expectation

_____

_____

Family expectations that have come true

_____

_____

HOME SWEET HOME

My Mother's House

Recently, I drove by the house I did most of my growing up in and found it altered, improved really, its face lifted and revealed. Stuff-shirted hedges had been stripped away and white paint sandblasted from the natural brick. Smart black trim flattered the bay windows.

An attractive renovation, hardly out of the ordinary, yet I stopped the car in stupid amazement. Had I thought the place immutable? Two families have lived there since mine left. Did I think my bedroom wallpaper was still there, airy nosegays, imagined bridal bouquets of my adolescent daydreams? I guess so. I stared at the door which was different, too, not the half-glass window through which I had peered into the kitchen, but an opaque slab.

Later, thinking about my stunned reaction, I realized that although I had been making a home of my own for twenty years, home, for me, in some way, is still behind the door to my mother's kitchen.

Once married, my first home-away-from-home was a furnished apartment most memorable for the bedroom that faced directly onto a parking lot a half-story below. At night the room was perpetually lit by the metallic glow of chrome shining in the moonlight. The only homey thing I can recall doing in that apartment was duplicating my mother's recipe for spaghetti sauce.

My mother, after coming for a visit and taking a smiling but investigative look around, promised to send me a present I really needed. It turned out to be an electric broom. There in the dust, it never occurred to me that I was making a home.

In the years that followed I felt more like I was playing house than setting up a household. Not settled in one place, with an attitude that presupposed permanency before real life could begin, I moved out of my twenties into apartment after apartment, never identifying myself with the term "housewife." As far as I could tell, real housewives knew how to sew and take care of wood floors; real mothers intuitively understood the enigma of colic and the subtleties of toilet training; real wives made social engagements and entertained on china. My wedding china remained packed away for safekeeping at my mother's. A real house.

None of the places I have lived in seem memorable to me in the same way my mother's house does. Of course, it's not a sentimental attachment to the bedroom with the flowered wallpaper or the big oak kitchen table that gives my memories their emotional edge. Feelings filled those rooms. I remember watching my father orchestrate those meals as head of a household where everyone knew their place. A safe place. I remember my mother making the rounds of goodnight kisses with wrap-around hugs and un-shy words of love. The feelings those rooms held remain sacred in my memory, and childhood memories, even if they are only loosely related to reality, tend to be permanent and immutable. My mother's house felt like a blanket I could wrap myself in. But now that I am the provider of that blanket in my own home, I never feel as though I am covering everything.

Over the years, I have learned that a home is not a natural state but a conscious invention. A home has an aura. We felt it as children, if we were lucky, but as adults, and women, for the most part, we must create that feeling with nothing to work with but our own resources. Every day. Paying the mortgage and putting food on the table are the cut and dried basics, but the rest, as far as I can tell is catching the ball and running with it. Curve ball, fly ball, or foul, it makes no difference. Once you're in the game, you can't drop it and walk off the field.

Sometimes, when you're standing ankle deep in water oozing from a broken washing machine, or waiting, ready for work, for the babysitter who never comes, you get a scary look at the scope of the effort you're involved in and it's easy to wish it away. Nevertheless, we keep right on trying to stretch that blanket of security over our houses even though we know they are in need of constant patching. Even though we know there are gaps in our goodwill, lapses in our initiative and limits to our patience. Even though we know nothing is certain and, despite our plans, we know what our mothers knew: that fate works in ways swifter and more mysterious than a microwave oven.

Yet we keep building the nest. We do it for ourselves and those depending on us: children, stepchildren, husband, even parents. Or maybe we do it *because* they are depending on us. Whether we work or not doesn't seem to matter. We are the psychological home base.

There was a long time when I felt as though I was always scrambling to get things back to normal, but then I discovered that a house with a repetitive series of crises, interruptions in anticipated plans, and disruptions in routine *was* normal. And it must have been the same at my mother's house. While she was holding her finger in the dike against chaos, I was leading a normal life. She shouldered the responsibilities, stocked the refrigerator, did the laundry, chauffeured me to all manner of life-enriching lessons, and picked up after me. "When you have your own house, you won't leave all your clothes on the chairs," she scolded me daily. She was right. But in my own house, I've never been quite as much at home as I was in hers.

Now my own children leave their clothes on the chairs (the floor, actually), and I hope they feel as much at home as I did then. They do tell me that they love this house we live in and look horrified if I mention moving. My younger daughter even hates to change the pictures on the wall, so she must be busy planting the seeds of permanent and immutable childhood memories. I like the house, too, am grateful for its comforts, but I don't adore its idio-syncracies. For instance, I know it eats money. I know that during the night all the creaks and groans I hear must be the house perversely thinking up ways to break down. Now at least, while I am its keeper, I don't feel the least bit senti-mental about it the way I do about the house I grew up in.

When I told my mother about the alteration of her old house, she replied with a polite but disinterested, "Oh, really."

Clearly, she doesn't miss that house the way I do. She's probably never even liked that flowered wallpaper. Perhaps, like me, the memories of home that are most real to her are those of her own mother's kitchen. Perhaps that's true of all of us.

The Red Crayon

---

*L*aundry is one of those household chores I like to do "in between." In between watching TV or working or *anything* rather than giving my full attention to that disheartening load of yesterday's clean clothes, dirty again. The only interesting thing about laundry is what comes out of its pockets.

If I'd saved every dime I've found, I'd never be without one to make a phone call again. To my mind, money that's gone through a full cycle of soap suds is washed clean of previous ownership. She who puts the laundry in, gets the money out.

My laundry is a regular lost and found—one earring, one barrette—halves of all kinds of pairs. My children are reluctant to ask if these missing partners have turned up because they know, whether their belongings have emerged or not, I'll bore them with a reprimand about taking care of their possessions. Evidently, it's less painful to lose something than to listen to my lecture.

I know laundry can produce evidence of behavior far more interesting than carelessness, but so far, I've never found anything really incriminating—no matchbooks from motels or papers with mysterious phone numbers. My discoveries run toward the mundane—fish hooks in the jackets of people who weren't supposed to be fishing; candy wrappers in the pockets of people who weren't supposed to be eating. Occasionally, school work appears folded into a nearly unbendable wad with a less than wonderful grade, soggy but still readable.

Once, my daughter left a red crayon in her pocket. It seems to have survived the washing machine because nothing came out even slightly pink. Perversely, it melted in the dryer. All over everything. Even my husband's underwear was pink. Everything white blushed.

Mostly, I saw red, but the rest of the family rallied to the child's defense. Her father said that it was about time he changed his style anyway, and her sister declared that the new purplish shade of her blue shirt was perfect. I even began to see the humor in the new tie-dyed look of my T-shirts.

That red crayon was certainly the high point of my laundry days. It's the only time I ever thought of laundry as a way to bring the family together.

The Dinner Table

*T*he dinner table has always seemed to me to be the family's historical center. I remember my own childhood mealtimes as a kind of friendly inquisition. My father sternly demanded an accounting of our days. "What happened in school?" he would ask. Without fail, he would be met with these banal responses: "Nothing," "Not much," and "We had a substitute." Annoyed, he would inquire again. We would deign to elaborate. The repetition of this scene never convinced anyone to improve their behavior. Practice never made perfect.

Once in a while, he would express his irritation with a dramatic pause. There would be a collective intake of breath. He would place his elbow on the table and deliberately point his fork at the child who had least pleased him. Then he would insist upon a more intelligible answer. The victim, prodded by a mingling of fear and respect, would produce a string of words hurriedly laced together and laded with the jargon of the day. He didn't understand *that* at all.

There were lighter moments, of course. We were all quick-witted and quick to laugh if we saw an opening in the tunnel of seriousness that made the dinner hour a "major family meeting." We teased each other unmercifully. No sensitive soul would have survived. We took our turns squirming, but we giggled a lot and laughed. And when the laughter took control of the table, when silliness had washed away a miserable day at the office, or a terrible moment at school, my father would joke along with us and call us "the looney tunes." He laughed the hardest of all.

Now my parents sit at my dinner table, and I am the questioner in charge. I quiz my children about their school days and am treated to the same maddening answers. Only the jargon has changed. Then I turn to my father and ask for an accounting: How does he feel? Did he rest? Sometimes I catch myself dramatically planting my elbow on the table and pointing at someone. And sometimes I feel as if I am witnessing an ending, although I know that's not true. There are no beginnings and endings, just family history repeating itself.

Somewhere Else

O n a scale of one to ten, I'd say my kids have a pretty good life. A room of their own, a room to play in, two dogs, a father who takes them fishing, and a mother who makes one outstanding chocolate chip cookie. I know better than to look for gratitude. But, really, I'm so tired of hearing about all those other terrific mothers and someone else's perfect home.

Evidently, there are mothers out there with culinary skill I've never come close to. What do they cook? Hot dogs! Charlotte's mom makes the best hot dog this side of the midwest, which is where she comes from. And maybe that's why. There must be a heartland knack to turning a hot dog on a grill that I can't duplicate. The same is true for brownies baked in someone else's oven and spaghetti prepared in another mother's kitchen. Superb! At a friend's house, my youngest child has even been known to eat stew, a meal that gives her visual indigestion at home—one look and she's sick. Rachel's mother makes *great* stew.

It's those negative comparisons that get to me. No one actually complains, not more than once and not after they've been told what they can do with their complaints, but they always manage to find something superior about somewhere else.

My older daughter recently went to a party in the *best* playroom she's ever been in. What was good about it? The mess. The few pieces of furniture were so demolished "you could do anything to them." That's a quote. The entire room, even the walls, was covered with ugly carpeting, so "you could do anything in there." That's another quote. I don't know what "anything" is because I was afraid to ask. I also didn't want to know why the new room we added to our house with its comfortable furniture, cozy rugs, cable TV and new stereo was old hat by comparison. Some things are better left unsaid.

Now that I think about it, I felt the same way about my mother's house when I was their age. But after I left home everything took a nostalgic turn for the better—my mother's cooking (except her stew), the den, even the oddly-decorated cellar where I held my parties. I imagine the same will happen to my children. Nothing here will really get any better, but their opinion will improve.

Taking our own homes for granted is like a childhood disease we all outgrow. But it's never too late to bring home a little appreciation. It will always be gratefully received.

Going Home

Many women I know go home for the holidays. On Thanksgiving, Christmas and Easter we pack up our families and go to our mother's or mother-in-law's. Even though we've been making homes for ourselves for years, acquired husbands, children, assorted animals, furniture, wallpaper, and gone through three sets of dishes, we still walk out the door and say we're going "home."

When, then, do our own houses become home? Strangely enough, it happens after the kids leave. During all those years of changing beds and changing scenes, of going from pinafores to prom dresses, we are busy building a nest for our children so that when they leave, off to schools or jobs, or off to their own houses or apartments, *they* will have a place to "go home" to for the holidays.

So Be It

I f you have no children," the old joke goes, "what do you do for aggravation." As a child I was sure that joke was inside out: my *parents* were the prickly part of the partnership, not me. But when I became a parent I recognized the message all too well. With children, irritation is knit right into the family fabric. Exasperation comes with the territory. But so does a child's laughter, that caressing sound that melts away anger and indignation and even sorrow. So if having children sometimes means pain, worry, and annoyance, so be it. The moments of aggravation are far outnumbered by the years of love.

Family Chores

*E*veryone in my house is in favor of family chores. There's only one problem. I seem to be the only one who understands the meaning of "neat and clean." Since I know they all mean well, maybe it's just a matter of communication. There is a lot of play in the words, "Keep your room neat." One person's mess may be another's lived-in look. But how neat is this? The dog got lost in my daughter's room. It's a big dog. The poor animal was backed into a corner by a pile of clothes that seemed to have a life of their own.

How about, "Keep your bathroom clean?" It seems I misinterpreted the soap scum and globs of toothpaste on the sink. I thought they were dirt, but my daughters corrected me. Soap and toothpaste, they explained, are things you clean *with*, not things you clean *up*. Now I understand.

I understand that all of us who are most responsible for the housework in any home just see the place through different eyes. Peeking into corners, we see dustballs; staring at the ceiling, we spy cobwebs. But if we want the whole family to pitch in and help, we'll probably have to avert our gaze and find a middle ground—somewhere between messy and immaculate—and be satisfied with a new definition of "neat and clean."

A Refrigerator Is Forever

*T*here's a cartoon which I adore. The picture is of two men meeting on the street and one greets the other with these words:

"So, how's the family? And all the major appliances?" How true, how true. On a scale of life's crucial considerations, the refrigerator ranks right up there behind the children. Kids grow up and leave home, but a refrigerator is forever.

Or so I thought. Mine turned out to be even less reliable than the children. After ten years of togetherness, I woke up one morning and the refrigerator just went up in flames. A fire in my refrigerator! Oh, it had been making a few complaining noises, a little whining and whirring. And I had anticipated, but frankly, had been ignoring, the possibility of some dripping or melting, intransigent behavior of some sort. But a fire? Now that is vicious. When I opened the door and saw that icebox filled with flames, boiling eggs and melting jelly, I knew it was all over between us.

My husband was out of town when the fire occurred, and I replaced the refrigerator before his return. No one in the family thought he would notice the difference. The man is one terrific eater, and the consensus was that he wouldn't care what his food was kept in as long as it was *there*. But we were wrong. He noticed right away and felt the loss. People can be very attached to their appliances and take mechanical breakdown as a real betrayal.

I'm afraid I took it personally when my refrigerator had the nerve to burn up. The inconvenience of a broken appliance is just an intolerable insult to my routine. Once I became unglued when my washing machine stopped running *during the wash cycle*. It was bad enough that I had no machine, but a tub full of dirty, soapy clothes was completely uncalled for.

I have functioned without a clothes dryer but in a climate so hot the garments dried practically as they were hung. Now I would do anything short of criminal to keep mine working. I must have been a much more rational person before I became so accustomed to the mechanical members of my family.

My appliances are so indispensable that I can't help but think of them as partners in the effort to keep a finger in the dike against the build-up of laundry, dust balls and garbage. I used to think that I was pretty independent, but now I know that without my refrigerator, washing machine, dryer, freezer, dishwasher, and probably even my disposal…I'm lost.

No matter how big or small, kitchens are the center of family life. Around the table, family business is conducted, heartbreaks are healed, problems are resolved, plans are discussed, and dreams take shape. The fire of family is kindled in the kitchen.

What I recall about my mother's kitchen

_____

_____

A kitchen I remember clearly

_____

_____

The kitchen I found most welcoming

_____

_____

Houses do indeed have personalities, although it often takes the people within to make them a home. Each house has an aura, an atmosphere, and idiosyncrasies lovingly created and, no doubt, treasured by its occupants. Houses frame our lives.

A memory that one house brings to mind

_____

_____

A room I felt good in

_____

_____

The "character" of one place I've lived

_____

_____

Nicknames can be amusing, affectionate, or maddening. But most are a form of fondness within the circle of family.

A child's pet name and its source

_____

_____

Nicknames my children used for each other

_____

_____

A nickname I had in my family

_____

_____

"Heirloom" is the word for anything handed down from one generation to the next, intrinsically valuable or not. A table or a teacup, heirlooms may not be fancy, but they are the visible evidence of a family's continuity.

Something I consider to be an heirloom

_____

_____

An heirloom that brings back fond memories

_____

_____

Something I'd like to pass to my children

_____

_____

When children step away from their parents, they often look back with a critical eye. This is a necessary part of growing up that requires patience and a sense of humor on the part of parents—because it is a time when their children have none.

The age my children began to see me as less than perfect

_____

_____

A ridiculous criticism of me

_____

_____

My reaction to a child's criticism

_____

_____

Give a child a chore and you'll get back an excuse.
Chores are something everyone does, but assigned
chores are tantamount to a curse—and, naturally,
children loathe them. A child will always work
hard to avoid a chore.

Chores we do as a family

_____

_____

Chores I give my children

_____

_____

Chores my children really dislike

_____

_____

Recreation is a family sport—what form it takes depends on the players. The basic requirements are patience on the part of parents and a willingness by the children to participate. Skill is beside the point. Having fun as a family is what matters most.

Sports I like to play with my children

_____

_____

Family activities the children enjoy most

_____

_____

Pastimes my children will take to adulthood

_____

_____

Family visits—between parents and their children, grandparents and grandchildren—are sometimes the only times spent together. They can be joyful, intense (and tense!), satisfying, and surprising. But they are always too short.

A family visit I especially remember

_____

_____

An amusing moment in a family visit

_____

_____

A visit I still want to make

_____

_____

LOVE
CONQUERS
ALL

"You Never Know"

$\mathcal{M}$y husband is a great collector of miscellaneous objects "that might come in handy some day." In the garage, there's a stack of tires, all the tires we've ever replaced on all our cars, which means they're very old. Old and worn. Asked why we keep them, he mumbles, "You never know," and, to him, that's a rational reply.

I guess you never know when you might need cleaner for the floor we ripped up six years ago, or stain for the deck two colors ago. A rake with three teeth is a mighty handy thing to have around, I suppose. There must be intrinsic or sentimental value in that garage full of misbegotten objects, but I can't find it. Or anything else I might really be looking for.

Every year before winter, I beg for car space in the garage and suggest, with only a speck of irony, that there might be some gems in there that have outlived their usefulness. I am perennially hopeful that something will have to be thrown out. Last year I had my eye on a bucket on wheels with an attachment that squeezes a string mop. My grandmother probably would have loved it, but I, for one, am never going to use it. My husband would rather dance with a mop than push one. But he found a place for it. The trouble is that each season he finds a place for everything. And still makes room for the car.

I've threatened and occasionally laid my hands on a few of these diamonds in the rough, but I've never actually thrown them out—the man is so *attached* to them. But when I think about it, he's probably attached to them the same way I'm connected to all those old belts in my closet that are too small. Not to mention the shoes that will never come back into style. And the skirts whose hemlines will never be right. But they might. You never know.

Universal Characteristic

Not all husbands are alike, of course, yet sometimes they share qualities that may not be inherently male, but seem to be acquired at the altar. Men bring varieties of goodness, kindness and tenderness to a marriage, but I've noticed one strangely universal characteristic. No husband I know accepts blame—that's his wife's job. And in case she forgets, he reminds her.

Just get in a car with your husband and get lost. Who is going to take the blame? No man I know. All husbands have a terrific sense of direction, and if they get lost, it's because their wives encouraged them to make a wrong turn. At such moments, the truth is irrelevant. The best thing is to keep your mouth shut, clenched actually, even if your teeth hurt.

Even though shifting the blame to your spouse appears nowhere in the wedding vows, it's everywhere in marriages. Especially when it comes to the children. Whenever children fall a mile or two below parental expectations, blame is usually placed on their mother's shoulders. Their father would never have let it happen. He would never have *allowed* it. He *knew* this was going to happen. Arguments in this case are futile. The poor man is just looking for a place to put his frustration and his wife is in a perfect position to take it.

Wives have even managed to take the blame for the house when it has the nerve to need repair. Why don't they *remind* their husbands to fix the faucet before water floods the kitchen, to cement the tiles before the floor comes up, to repair the screens before the bugs move in? Why? Because they don't want to be blamed for nagging, I guess.

None of this is intentional. Good men, kind and considerate husbands, are as guilty (pardon the expression) of this behavior as anyone else. And their wives, for some reason that is probably inspired at the altar, too, allow them their way. So can you blame them?

Gone Fishing

My husband is an outdoorsman. He was raised in the great outdoors of suburbia but, for no reason that anyone in his family can discern, his heart beats best in the woods. Fishing, especially in remote rivers and streams, is his passion. His other devotion is his family and, from the very beginning, he was determined to reconcile the two.

When he married me, the wildest place I'd been was the tallest grass on a golf course. It's called "the rough" but, believe me, it isn't. I am not an outdoorsman, but my husband took me everywhere and he tried, he really did, to teach me the skill and pleasure that he so enjoys. I *can* fish and *have* fished with him in rivers, streams, oceans, lakes, ponds, wherever there's water bigger than a puddle.

But it turns out that I have no talent for it. He patiently sets me up with the necessary equipment and a good spot and then leaves me alone to become a fishing fiasco. My line tangles; my reel screeches; my waders leak. I catch perch when trout are what we're after; tuna when sailfish is the prize. I lack the soul of a fisherman.

I do love to go with him, though, but the truth is, it's the places, not the fish, that draw me: beaches at dawn and twilight, and rivers where the water churns over rocks and tap dances in the sun. I just want to *be* there. Give me a book, a candy bar and, oh yes, a fishing rod, and I am content.

My older daughter, as it happens, is like her mother, a lover of vistas and sunsets. But with my younger daughter, my husband got lucky. As soon as she was tall enough to stand in water, she began to fish with a seriousness of purpose that can only be hereditary. Recognizing her inclination, her father set out to develop it and that meant taking precious time from his own fishing, time he counted in hours that were always too few. But he never gave up. He lost whole fishing-days dragging her out of the water when she fell in, coming back when she was cold, or leaving early when, as she got older, she had homework or other plans. Once she cut an entire trip short by hooking herself in the scalp. But he keeps on taking her.

Of course, he has other people to fish with, other men and even me with my book. But that wouldn't be the same. When you share something you love with your children, no one else can take their place.

Opposites Attract

I am very neat. That's not a virtue, just a fact. My children say it's pathological, but I think it's just a trait inherited from my father who's been nicknamed "Mr. Neat Man" by his grandchildren and called a "neat freak" behind his back. There are claims that he folds his dirty laundry before stacking it (edges aligned) in the hamper, but no actual witnesses. So I grew up with the idea that men, in general, know how to hang towels on a rack in perfectly symmetrical order. I was deluded.

My husband thinks a wet towel is an object worthy of a place on the bathroom floor—which is where he leaves it. I was a surprised bride. After a while, I became a nagging wife. When that didn't work, I picked up the towels. And put away the shaving cream, the cup, the hair brush and the toothpaste. And that's only the bathroom.

My mother always told me that, to make a marriage work, wives have to give sixty percent and husbands, forty. I'm still not sure exactly what she meant, but I figure I'm contributing my extra twenty percent in sweeping up tobacco, picking up newspapers, and hanging up clothes. And it's not so bad. There are a lot of worse ways to contribute to a marriage than taking banana peels out of ashtrays.

So we go on as we began. I compose my napkin into compulsive little squares. He scrunches his into a mangled mess. He packs for a trip like he's fleeing the country. I pack as if I'm expecting a military inspection. His drawers are full of strangled clothes. My underwear is folded with hospital corners.

Two clichés apply here because better words are yet to be invented: opposites attract and love conquers all.

Marriage may be a 50-50 arrangement, but having a family requires giving more than 100 percent—everyday. The effort may be enormous but the return is immeasurable.

A new emotion I found in having a family

_____

_____

A form of giving I had not experienced before

_____

_____

Rewards of family life

_____

_____

Sometimes there are people with whom we are so intimately involved that they become part of our families. Because these relationships are purposeful, not an accident of birth, they are all the more precious.

Friends who are "family" to my children

_____

_____

The qualities that make these people part of our family

_____

_____

An "uncle" or "aunt" I loved as a child who was not a relative

_____

_____

A family is a link between the past and the future. There is much in the past that we hope our children will value and carry into their futures. It is a parent's role to make the connection.

A family value I have tried to instill in my children

_____

_____

A family tradition I hope my children will keep

_____

_____

Something that I would like to see preserved

_____

_____

Relationships between siblings can be calm or explosive, devoted or detached. Where there are brothers and sisters there is sure to be tumult. Making the mix work is the art of being a family.

How my kids get along

_____

_____

Why my children are close (or not close)

_____

_____

The way I hope my children will relate to their siblings as adults

_____

_____

The frustration and triumph of teaching a child a new skill are central to family life. The sense of accomplishment in learning to ride a bike, swing a bat, or swim a race, is a joy for both parents and children.

A skill I taught my children

_____

_____

An ability they learned on their own

_____

_____

A special memory I have of a child
mastering a skill

_____

_____

Young people who date do not think of themselves as children anymore, as their parents do. There is no resolution for this situation. Growing up is one of those inevitable facts of life that children long to hasten and parents want to postpone.

My feelings about my child's first "date"

_____

_____

Changes in my children dating has brought

_____

_____

Changes in our relationship

_____

_____

Parents who stand in line waiting for gratitude are going to be there for awhile. It's not likely to be coming—at least not in any well-defined way. But children do feel appreciative—you just have to look into their hearts.

Moments when I feel appreciated

_____

_____

A small way in which my children say thank you

_____

_____

What I am grateful for

_____

_____

Family pride grows out of experience and effort, small victories, and satisfying achievements. But there is also pride in family members for just being themselves, and for building and sustaining a vital, loving family.

A reason I am proud of my family

_____

_____

Something I want my children to be proud of

_____

_____

Why I am proud of myself

_____

_____

FAMILY
TIES

Well-organized Heredity

*T*he apple, my father tells me, "doesn't fall far from the tree." Some people may wonder what he's talking about, but not me. Once you've grown up within earshot of a family's peculiar vernacular, you always know not only what's being said, but who's doing the talking. All families are alike in this regard, only the rhetoric differs.

"The apple doesn't fall far from the tree" is my father's definitive comment on how similar my behavior is to my mother's. The more absent-minded, dithering, or noodle-brained he thinks I behave, the more he goes on about apples and trees. I take some comfort in the thought that heredity is so well-organized.

No one I know other than my Aunt Lillie makes this remark: "I'm so busy I don't know whether I'm on foot or horseback!" That woman will run that sentence by anybody who'll listen any time of the day. Actually, she doesn't need anybody to listen. Besides, everybody in the family knows she "doesn't know which end is up," her alternate phrase when she's really rushed.

One refrain of my mother's echoes through my adolescence. She always got a kick out of teenage romances, the odd pairings of my girlfriends and boyfriends. It was the choices that tickled her, the incongruous couples that chemistry cooked up. She'd shake her head and chuckle, "That's what makes horse racing." Indeed. Sometimes she would add, "There's a Jack for every Jill," but by that time she'd lost her audience.

My mother said and so do I: "All I want is some peace and quiet!" I never thought I'd hear those words coming out of my mouth, but there they are, rolling right off my tongue when the occasion arises. The one thing I've learned about who says what is that it's bound to be repeated by the next generation.

Family

There's something irresistible about relatives. Even when they are related more by blood than inclination, even when they are separated by time and distance, they remain, somehow, "family."

There are relatives who might never have chosen to speak three words to one another, yet they are inextricably tied up in the same family knot. Less than strangers, more than friends, they are drawn together in the magnetic field of the family. And under these peculiar circumstances, a kind of connectedness flourishes.

Uncles and aunts take pleasure in nieces and nephews simply because they are children of their own siblings. And cousins develop an affectionate unit all their own in spite of the fact that they may have nothing in common but their parents' relationships. The bond of shared heredity is so strong that even distant relatives that are out of sight and out of mind can never really be *un*related. Curiosity, if nothing else, keeps them connected. You can't saw a limb off the family tree.

Uncle Archie

$\mathcal{E}$very Sunday my Uncle Archie came to visit. My father was usually out for a while involved in one sport or another. But my uncle, who owned a dairy, had to work for a few hours and, on his way home, he would stop to see my mother, his baby sister. As far as I was concerned, my mother had never been *anyone's* little sister. Besides, I thought Uncle Archie came to see me and bring me ice cream, which he did.

So while the ice cream kept me occupied, my mother and her brother could talk without interruption. I was too young to be interested in what they said, but what I remember now is the tone. In their voices I heard the connectedness of siblings, the pleasure of hearing in each other's words a lifetime of meaning, the joy of seeing in each other's faces the child who became the adult. For a little while, they must have felt their lives whole, the continuum from youth to maturity unbroken.

I couldn't be put off for too long, of course, and Uncle Archie never disappointed me. I would climb onto his lap and we would play a game that can only be called, "Deedle, Dum, Dum, Dum." He would bounce me up and down and sing a little "deedle dum" tune. At an unexpected, but thrillingly-anticipated moment, he would let me slip between his knees and then scoop me up before I hit the floor. It was the most fun. He would hug me and call me his "Apple." When my sister was born, she became his "Peach." But I know now that the real apple of his eye was my mother, his baby sister.

Little Brother

I was the oldest of three children, a fact that provided me with the privileges of rank and a permanent job— babysitting without pay. My sister was seven and my brother, three, when I was left home alone with them in the evening for the first time. I was eleven, and my mother thought I was ready. She was half right. Half the night I spent in the den watching TV where I was fine. For the other half, I needed a chaperone.

I was afraid to walk by the dining room where the curtains on the big bay window had been left open, exposing me to the goblins of suburbia. So I crawled— to and from the kitchen, up the stairs, everywhere that dreaded eye of night could see me. My little brother crawled right along beside me—precision crawling. Either he thought it was a game or he was afraid to let me out of his sight. When my parents came home, they found all three of us in one bedroom, my sister asleep in her bed and my brother and I in mine.

But that was nothing new. My sister and I shared a room and my brother had his own across the hall—very blue and masculine with decorative trains charging around the walls. In his bed beneath the locomotives, he was lonely. Often, during the night, he crept down the long, scary corridor to my parents' room hoping for an invitation to join them. But my mother and father had already gone that route with two older children and were not real receptive to a third child sneaking up to their bed, staring at them until they awoke, startled into expecting disaster. And that's how my brother ended up in my bed.

He would slip into our room in the dark, a curly-headed toddler wired with fear of the mysterious strangers in his dreams. I was eight years older than he but only slightly removed from those primeval terrors myself. So, sleepily sympathethic, I made room for him under the covers. Unfortunately, the more used to my sympathy he became, the more room he took up. After I spent several months sleeping with my face creased on the edge of the mattress, we developed a routine. He would wake me up and I would say, "Get your own pillow," which he did. He never came without his pillow. That was against the rules. Permission first, pillow second.

I think his nocturnal visits ended when his dreams became more bearable than my sister's teasing. But for a long time after that, I would wake up mornings and find him sitting between my sister's bed and mine playing with his toys, content with our sleeping companionship.

When my brother got married, after an extended bachelorhood, I was particularly pleased. All those years I had worried about him. He was never meant to have a room of his own.

Great-Aunt Lena

*M*y great-aunt Lena was my mother's saviour and practically a saint to me, even when I was eight years old. Whenever my parents went on vacation, throughout my childhood, Aunt Lena came to take care of my little sister, brother and myself. To say she "came" is to imply half her sainthood.

She managed to cross the length of Brooklyn by subway, descending and ascending flights and flights of unforgiving concrete steps. She managed to untangle the maze at Grand Central and board a train, disembark, climb more stairs and catch a bus that brought her, with just a few more blocks to walk, to our door. She had come to the country—Connecticut was, in her mind, the country—to help her niece. And why not? She loved her.

We loved it when Aunt Lena came but we hated when our mother went away. Taking this back-handed compliment without offense, she helped us to handle our tangled emotions by filling up the hours with games and projects. She tolerated the most tedious card games with good nature, but her favorite was Old Maid. Somehow, after incredible twists of fate and heartstopping suspense, the doomed Old Maid card ended up in her hands. "Boo hoo, boo hoo," she would cry, "I'm the Old Maid, boo hoo, boo hoo." "No you're not, no you're not!" we'd insist, squirming into her lap, draping over her shoulders, climbing up her arms. And she always seemed to have plenty of lap and bosom and arms for a child to wrap herself in even though she wasn't a large woman.

I thought Aunt Lena terrifically different. Wearing her salt-and-pepper hair in tight braids across her head, peasant style, she took it down only at night when I remember her barefoot in her nightgown with a great mane of braid-frizzled gray and black and white hair surrounding her face. Elegant, broad cheek bones and a high forehead were her most prominent features—interrupted by jet black eyes. I thought she was too old to be beautiful.

When I was a teenager, Aunt Lena was still coming to the door and we had our best times together. Keeping track of all my friends, their rivalries and romances, she wanted to know all the Gothic details of our adolescent loves, and she seemed to relate directly to each heart-rending trauma, never taking an attitude of increased wisdom with her years.

"You know," she would say, "I don't feel any different from when I was nineteen. The body changes," she sighed, "but inside I still feel the same." I tried to imagine her as a girl of nineteen with long black braids and high rounded cheeks with no lines to define them, but I couldn't.

In her mid-sixties, Aunt Lena modernized, cut her then white hair and wore it swept away from her forehead and cheeks, now smooth high circles etched in wrinkles. Having become a matriarch in the family, she kept in touch with four generations, inundating the post office with birthday and anniversary cards and still appearing at the doors of those who needed her.

At 69 she met a man, a widower whose generosity

and sweetness of soul matched hers. When they were married, the family came from everywhere, a few of them were children and grandchildren, but most of us were nieces and nephews and we came not out of duty, but out of love. Today her affection has still not found its limit in her husband's large family, six children, 16 grandchildren and a bevy of nieces and nephews. The post office is busier than ever. We always knew she was never really the Old Maid.

Grandmothers

*M*y mother-in-law is a teacher, and there's no doubt in my mind that the lucky first-graders who sat in front of her blackboard learned how to read. As a young woman she had more glamorous aspirations, but life's necessities brought her into the professon she was born for. By now, there must be adults scattered all over the country who arc grateful for their school year with her. As a talented teacher, she was a gift.

As a grandmother/teacher, she is a treasure. By the time my children were old enough to come under her loving tutelage, she was retired, but only from the classroom. A teacher as much by instinct as training, she simply went on providing learning experiences to whatever children were at hand and mine were fortunate enough to be handy.

In her view, every event, any ordinary activity, was an opportunity for them to learn something. But her teaching was so gentle, so tempered with humor and patience, that the kids thought they were just having fun. Questioning them, leading them step by step, she brought them to the brink of discovery—and then, with hugs and laughter, she cheered *their* quickness and cleverness. The fact that they gained pride in themselves and a sense of accomplishment was no accident either. She taught them more than information.

Part of her secret, I think, is that she always spoke to them in just the right tone, never addressing them as babies or merely short adults. She spoke to them as children with intelligence, and, to my amazement, that's how they responded.

When the children were quite young she moved away. But she kept up a correspondence packed with information about the flora and fauna of her new location. Sending newspaper clippings and pictures, she made her instructive presence felt even in her absence. Once the kids received a map of the world so big we couldn't find a wall to hang it on. If there had been no letter enclosed, they still would have known who sent it.

Since visits were infrequent, I was afraid she might lose her special touch with her grandchildren, but I needn't have worried. Adjusting her level of instruction as they grew, she even found something to captivate their adolescent attention. With a little editing, she told them all about their father when he was a teenager and that is one fascinating piece of information they couldn't have acquired from anyone else.

Children will listen and learn for just so long, of course, and then they approach the age when they think they are the ones who know everything. But grandmothers are wise enough not to be surprised or offended. They've been through that stage with one generation already.

Sisters Are Special

I have only one sister and when I was a youngster I thought that was enough. Four years younger than I, interested in toys when I was enamored with boys, silly when I became sophisticated, she wasn't exactly a pest, but not a pleasure either. We shared a room, a set of parents, and the same piano teacher, and except for that, I thought we had nothing in common. The four year gap seemed too hard to bridge.

I was wrong. After a certain age, four years seem to

lose their length. For some reason, the eternity between twelve and sixteen is nothing like the four years I experience today. When I was sixteen I thought being older was better, and I did have some advantages—a curfew past 11:00, a driver's license, and a boyfriend—all the important things in life. Now, the only advantage I have is advanced knowledge of the aging process, and there's no point in sharing that information with my sister. She'll find out soon enough for herself.

But we share nearly everything else. We have in common those habits and idiosyncracies that could only come from growing up in the same home. Open either of our cupboards and you will find nearly all the same foods, and even the same brands, stacked in about the same order. We are both mildly obsessive about keeping the kitchen floor clean, emptying wastebaskets and throwing out old magazines. Since these are hardly biologically inherited traits, we must have acquired them by osmosis in our mother's house. We cook and keep house so similarly that when one of us goes out of town and leaves our children with the other, the kids barely notice the difference.

Our opinions are so close that if she agrees with me, I feel affirmed, but if she challenges my decisions, I reconsider. If she tells me I've insulted my husband, berated my children for no reason, or been too harsh with my dog, I apologize to everybody. No one else would tell me these things. Probably no one else would have the nerve. But I can count on my sister to tell me what I need to know.

Being born into the same household certainly doesn't guarantee this kind of relationship. And sometimes complicated family histories obscure the fact that sisters are very special. But if you think back to the time when you were just sisters, no one's wife or mother or daughter-in-law, you'll see that no one knows you quite like your sister does.

Cowlicks

---

*O*ne of the things I like most about relatives is that they remember me when I had a ponytail—and when all the rest of me was pretty perky too. That may be a selfish reason for liking someone, but some days, the idea feels so good I just enjoy it. Of course, if they can recall my ponytail, small waist, and my face before lines gave it character, I know they can remember the years I wore braces on my teeth, too. But that's OK. Families love to trace the changes that turn all of us into revised versions of our predecessors.

Naturally, none of us can see it ourselves. That's what we have relatives for. They're the only ones with the inside information to know. I've been told, for example, that I have my mother's laugh and my father's smile. Here are two inseparable characteristics and yet they are readily distinguished by anyone in the family who knows the sound of that laugh and the curve of that smile. So it must be true. I also have my mother's funny toes, but so far, no one has noticed.

Like all children, I was embarrassed by this affectionate scrutinization, but now I can't help but do it myself. And help but get carried away. I stop people in the middle of conversations to tell them how much their expression is like their mother's. When I see a father's cowlick appear in the same spot on his son's head, I can't take the miracle for granted. I am astounded over and over by the simple transmission of family traits. And thrilled, too, because in those expressions and cowlicks and toes is undeniable evidence that every generation is linked to those that follow.

A Family Kind of Feeling

Family occasions, weddings, birthdays, anniversaries, not to mention Thanksgiving, Christmas and Easter, can crowd a person's calendar. They can also put a damper on the purported joy of giving. What can you buy for a sixteen-year-old niece who dresses like a rock star and reads computer manuals for fun? Just where do her interests lie—in make-up or modems? And what can you give to a newborn whose mother plans for the child to be organically grown? Is there anything made for a baby without polyester or plastic?

Just getting to these celebrations can be an ordeal. One member of my family chose to be married on the Fourth of July at a place directly on route to the largest beach in the state. Memories of that wedding fester on for those of us who inched our way there in the melting traffic.

People do refuse such invitations, make excuses, respond with regrets. But I've been taught from an early age that if the pleasure of my company is requested, I'm supposed to attend. I learned my lesson listening to my grandmother who took every invitation as a command performance and a reward for having lived long enough to enjoy the maturing of others. She kept the family social register and knew the roster of everyone's coming events.

To her, family gatherings were not just parties, but ceremonies, rituals to mark life's milestones. Their inherent joys were her sustenance, and she wanted us all to appreciate their value.

So when her children and grandchildren expressed reluctance because they thought their personal time was more precious than time spent with the family at large, she simply disregarded their remarks. She would look placidly at the misguided among us and then conclude the discussion as if there had been no argument.

"So, you'll come," she would say regally, knowing she had the authority of righteousness on her side. And no one could refuse.

And after the graduation or the wedding, after we'd talked about *everyone*, taken stock of the family characters, commented on every new hairdo and old spouse, we were glad that we had gone. Attending *was* important, although that realization usually came with the long view rather than the day itself. Since my grandmother's view had the length of years, she knew that every one of those events was an occasion to strengthen the strands of her family web. And she wasn't going to miss a single chance.

All family gatherings are celebrations, I think, whatever the occasion. The value of coming together is more than worth the trip.

A holiday recipe, a decoration, a tree ornament — these are the sweet details that add up to family traditions. Children raised on traditions ultimately bring them to their own families, linking the past to the future.

A holiday tradition I continued from
my own family

_____

_____

One thing that has become a tradition
in our family

_____

_____

A tradition I hope my children will carry on
in their families

_____

_____

Sunday morning pancakes? Friday night movies at home? There are rituals in every household that mark the rhythm of family life. Small occasions and intimate moments are the beating of the family heart.

Habits that draw the family together

_____

_____

Rituals I like most

_____

_____

What I contribute to these gatherings

_____

_____

Family history, like history on a grander scale, keeps repeating itself. Personality traits and physical characteristics emerge in successive generations, keeping family heritage alive. How special it is to see ourselves in our children and our grandchildren.

A trait that one of my children shares with a grandparent

_____

_____

A good quality that a child inherited from a parent

_____

_____

A family tendency that I hope will always remain

_____

_____

In the family tree, cousins are the valuable outer limbs. They broaden our involvement in the family's life.

The "outer branch" of the family I am closest to

_____

_____

A cousin I particularly like

_____

_____

Reasons I like to keep in touch with cousins

_____

_____

_____

_____

Events like graduations and weddings gather together the outer members of the family circle. Everyone who attends is not just a celebrant but a witness to the important passages in a family's history.

An event that was particularly important to the life of the family

_____

_____

A gathering I remember with special fondness

_____

_____

What I hope for the next family celebration

_____

_____

Family ties are very elastic these days, stretching across continents and even oceans. A family that is flexible will not break, but pull together in love and affection.

Distant places some family members live

_____

_____

A family member I miss because of distance

_____

_____

A place where I wish we could all live

_____

_____